Take a trip to

FINLAND

Keith Lye

General Editor
Henry Pluckrose

Franklin Watts

London New York Sydney Toronto

Facts about Finland

Area:
337,032 sq. km.
(130,129 sq. miles)

Population:
4,901,000 (1986 estimate)

Capital:
Helsinki

Largest cities:
Helsinki (922,000)
Tampere (248,000)
Turku (244,000)
Espoo (145,000)

Official languages:
Finnish, Swedish

Religion:
Christianity (Lutherans,
90 percent)

Main exports:
Paper and paperboard,
machinery and transport
equipment, wood and
wood pulp, ships

Currency:
Markka

Franklin Watts Limited
12a Golden Square
London W1

ISBN: UK Edition 0 86313 334 7
ISBN: US Edition 0 531 10104 5
Library of Congress Catalog
Card No: 85 51581

© Franklin Watts Limited 1986

Typeset by Ace Filmsetting Ltd,
Frome, Somerset
Printed in Hong Kong

Maps: Tony Payne
Design: Arthur Brown
Stamps: Stanley Gibbons Limited
Photographs: Finnish Tourist Board;
Zefa, 3, 4, 6, 7, 13, 14, 15, 17, 24, 27;
Finnish Embassy, 18, 19, 20, 21, 23; Paul
Forrester, 8
Front cover: Finnish Tourist Board
Back cover: Zefa

Finland is a large country in northern Europe. Winters are long, cold and snowy, especially in the north. People called Lapps live in the far north, where snow covers the land from October to April. Lapps use reindeer to draw their sleds.

Finland has more than 55,000 lakes and forests cover more than two-thirds of the land. Many city dwellers own country cottages. Many cottages have a special kind of bath, called a sauna, built alongside them. Saunas are extremely hot rooms, where people perspire freely. Most Finns take a sauna bath at least once a week.

Because of Finland's northern position, summer days are long, but winter days are short even in the southern Åland Islands. Places north of the Arctic Circle have at least one day a year when the Sun does not set. This is the Land of the Midnight Sun.

Finland is a republic. The Head of State is the President, who is elected to six-year terms. The President appoints the Prime Minister, who chooses the Cabinet. The Parliament in Helsinki, shown here, consists of only one house with 200 elected members.

Helsinki, in the far south, became Finland's capital in 1812. It is an important port on the Gulf of Finland. This gulf is an arm of the Baltic Sea. It freezes over for three to five months every year.

The picture shows some stamps and money used in Finland. The main unit of currency is the markka, which contains 100 pennia.

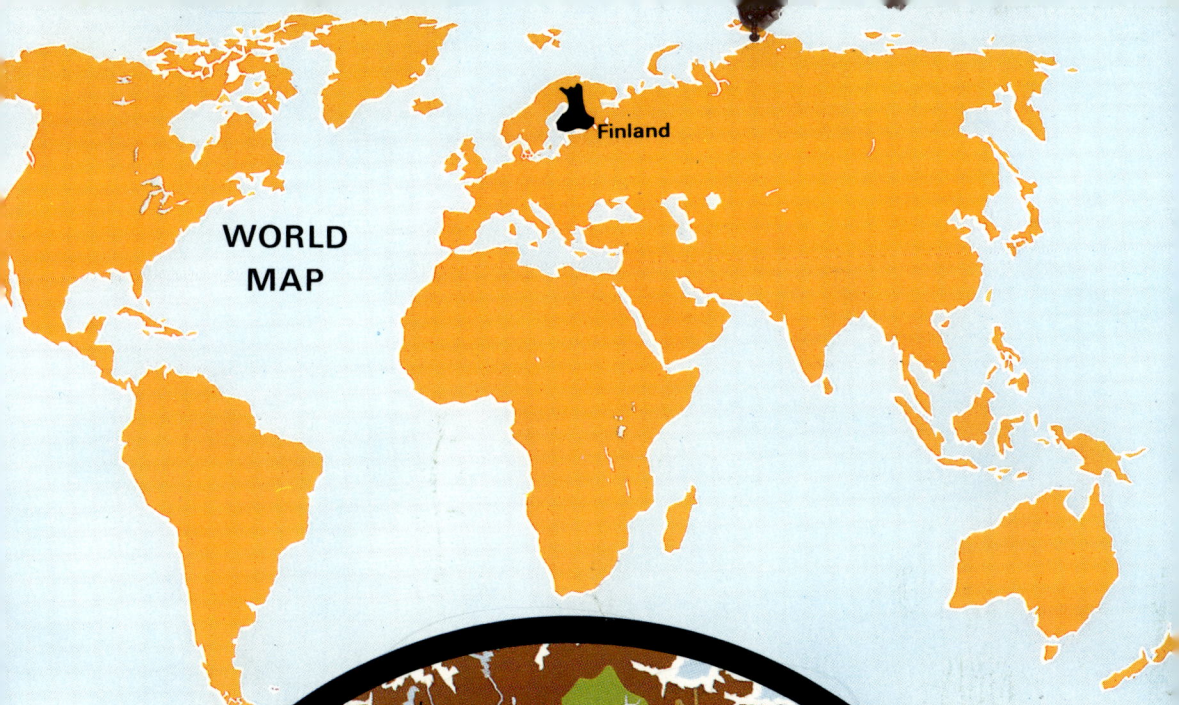

WORLD MAP

Finland

NORWAY

LAPLAND

SWEDEN

Rovaniemi

Kemi

Oulu

GULF OF BOTHNIA

Jakobstad

FINLAND

U.S.S.R.

Vaasa

Kuopio

Jyväskylä

Pori

Tampere

Savonlinna

Lahti

Turku

Kotka

Åland Is.

Helsinki

Espoo

GULF OF FINLAND

9

Finland has had a complicated history. It was ruled by Sweden for hundreds of years. The Swedes made Turku, shown here, the capital city. But Russia also claimed Finland and fought many wars with Sweden for control of the country.

This castle, built in Savonlinna in southeastern Finland in 1475, helped to protect the country's eastern borders. However, Finland became part of Russia in 1809. Finland declared its independence from Russia in 1917 and became a republic in 1919.

Over 90 out of every 100 people are of Finnish descent, but 7 out of every 100 speak Swedish as their native language. Finland is prosperous and most Finns enjoy a high standard of living. This market is in Helsinki.

The Lapps in northern Finland number less than 5,000. Most of these short, sturdy people lead a wandering life, following reindeer herds. Some live in tents made from reindeer skins. Winter tents are often made of wool.

13

The Swedes introduced Christianity into Finland. In 1540, they made Lutheranism the official religion and nine out of every ten people now belong to the Evangelical Lutheran Church. This wooden church is in Jakobstad on the west coast.

Russia introduced the Eastern Orthodox religion into Finland. Today, about one out of every 100 people belongs to the Finnish Orthodox Church. The picture shows the Orthodox Cathedral in Helsinki. It was built in 1868, when Russia ruled Finland.

Finlandia Hall in Helsinki was designed by a great Finnish architect, Alvar Aalto. *Finlandia* is the name of a piece of music by Finland's greatest composer, Jean Sibelius. Written in 1900, it became the anthem of Finns who wanted to be independent of Russia.

Finland is one of Europe's most thinly populated countries. About 64 out of every 100 people live in cities and towns. The picture shows Tampere, the second largest city, in south-central Finland. It stands on a short river that connects two big lakes.

17

Finland's forests are sometimes called green gold, because they are the country's chief resource. Valuable trees include pine, spruce and birch. Here a forester is cutting off the branches from a felled tree.

18

Logs are often taken from the forests to nearby rivers and lakes. There, foresters tie them into rafts, which are floated or towed to sawmills. Felled trees are replaced by seedlings.

Wood has many uses. Some is pulped and made into paper and paperboard. Finland ranks seventh in the world in producing these items. It is also the fourth largest producer of newsprint, the paper used for newspapers.

The country's name in Finnish is Suomi, which means lakeland. Many rivers and lakes have been dammed. At these dams, hydroelectric power stations produce about a third of the electricity used in Finland.

Finland produces some copper, iron ore and other metals. It has a wide variety of manufacturing industries including shipbuilding, seen in this picture. Mining and manufacturing employ 35 out of every 100 workers.

Finland is known for its designers, who make beautiful glassware, pottery, stainless steel eating utensils and many other products. Many of these items are exported and sold in other countries.

Farms cover nearly one-tenth of Finland. The chief crops are cereals, including barley, oats and wheat, potatoes and hay. Farming, forestry and fishing together employ 11 out of every 100 workers. Finnish farmers use modern machinery.

Most of Finland's farms are small and they are concentrated in the southwest where the climate is mildest. Dairy farming and livestock rearing provide four-fifths of the value of Finland's farm production.

In July and August, people enjoy outdoor activities. After the long winter, the summer sun is very welcome. These Finns are attending an open-air music festival. Rock and pop music, jazz, opera and symphonic music are all popular.

Folk music and dancing are kept alive by young Finns. They perform in traditional costumes at annual festivals, such as Midsummer's Eve, and on many other occasions.

Finnish children learn how to ski at an early age. The most popular type of skiing is cross-country skiing. Schools give children a 10-day skiing holiday in winter. Finns also enjoy ice skating and ice hockey.

The kitchen is the hub of life in many Finnish homes. Popular snacks include coffee with pastries and open sandwiches. Reindeer meat, fish, pork pies and crayfish are among the special dishes made in Finland.

Christmas is an important family festival. It is especially exciting when Santa Claus brings presents in his reindeer-drawn sled. Children give food to birds at Christmas, because snow covers the land.

The Finns are healthy, athletic people. They are famed as long distance runners, gymnasts and swimmers. In summer, they also enjoy surfing and sailing on the lakes and at coastal resorts.

Index

32